LANDSCAPES OF
SCOTLAND

1378
This edition published 1993
© 1985 Coombe Books
ISBN 0 86283 335 3
Printed and bound in Singapore by Tien Wah Press

LANDSCAPES OF
SCOTLAND

COOMBE BOOKS

Scotland and England have been ruled by the same monarchy, and governed by the same parliament, for well over 250 years. The inhabitants of both countries speak the same language and use the same currency. They don't need passports or visas to move from one country to the other and there are no customs posts on the border.

Yet when most Englishmen cross the border into Scotland there is a very definite feeling of entering a foreign country. It is the "Scottishness" of Scotland that sets any first-time visitor back on his heels.

"You see it in the architecture," says Michael Powell in *Alastair MacLean's Scotland* (Deutsch 1972), "in the colossal granite walls of Aberdeen, in the majestic sweep into the heart of Dundee of the road bridge over the Tay, in the fantasies of Scottish baronial, in the purity of the Brothers Adam. You hear it in the speech – direct, literate and colorful – whether broad Lowland or careful Highland. You enjoy it in the abundance of public golf courses; the stupendous high teas; the generous drams of whisky; the electric blankets on the clean beds; the unpretentious goodness of the small things in life."

You see it, too, in the breathtaking sweep of a Highland glen, where the thin winding ribbon of gray road creeping almost apologetically through it seems a concession of nature to man's intrusion. The delicate hues of bracken and heather on either side of the road are broken by a mountain stream that was bubbling when Scotland had its own kings, and a Sassenach Englishman took his life in his hands if he crossed the border.

It is the Scots themselves who have given their land this unique sense of identity – no mean achievement for a country of just over five million people.

It has been argued that the Scots have produced more eminent figures per capita than any other people. More than half the total number of American Presidents have Scottish ancestry and many British Prime Ministers have been Scots: Macmillan, Douglas-Home, Gladstone, Ramsay MacDonald. Menzies of Australia and Fraser of New Zealand also had Scottish blood and John Paul Jones, founder of the U.S. Navy, was a Scot. And in many other fields, Scots are internationally acclaimed; Andrew Carnegie, Adam Smith, James Watt, Robert Burns and Sir Walter Scott, to name but a few.

But the irony is that so many Scots achieved their success after leaving their homeland, making their mark on the world in foreign fields.

Alastair MacLean, the best-selling novelist, himself an expatriate, believes that his fellow countrymen are "born adventurers.... Find a man herding sheep in the furthest reaches of Patagonia and the chances are that he is a Scot. I know of a village in the Italian Dolomites where the most commonly held surnames begin with 'Mac'.... The Scots are to be found virtually everywhere." (*Alastair MacLean's Scotland*).

But where did the Scots come from originally? Most historians agree that the first man to stand upright on the rugged terrain of what is now Scotland did so perhaps as long ago as 6,000 BC. Bone and antler fishing spears and other rudimentary implements found mainly along the western part of the country serve as evidence to support this theory.

The Beaker civilization arrived three thousand years later, and is notable for its henges (of which Stonehenge is one of the most famous). The Beaker people eventually spread as far north as Orkney.

It was not for another 1,500 years or so that the first signs of Scotland's Celtic origins appeared. Around 500 BC the sparse population was roughly divided into two distinct areas. In the north and west, living in "duns" and "brochs", were the non-Celtic people who became known as Picts. To the south and east, mainly in hill forts and camps, lived the Celtic Britons. One of their chief settlements was Din Eidyn (Edinburgh).

The Roman Invasion of Britain isolated the two peoples even further. The Britons capitulated before the Roman legions and over the years of the occupation learned to work with them. The Picts, however, never bowed to Rome and even Hadrian's Wall was not strong enough to keep them from attacking the settlements to the south. As the Roman grip weakened, toward the end of the fourth century, their forces abandoned any hope of suppressing the Picts and, instead, appointed local Briton chiefs to uphold the law, such as it was.

The Irish Connection
But the Picts and the Britons were not the forerunners of the Scots of today. Scotland's heritage, in fact, came from Ireland in the sixth century, with an exodus of Gaels looking for fresh pastures. They landed in Argyll and, when the Irish St. Columba followed a few years later to hoist the flag of Christianity on the British mainland for the first time, the seeds of Scotland's future were planted.

St. Columba established his monastery on the island of Mull and for more than 30 years, until his death in 597, worked tirelessly to spread the Gospel. In doing so, he was instrumental in forging a unity among the people that would later take the shape of a national identity.

Before this could materialize, however, a new threat arrived on Scottish shores: Norse invaders, the most frightening war machine of its time. For more than 200 years the land was decimated by Viking raiders and much of St. Columba's work was destroyed. Even the fiercely independent Picts were no match for them. In fact, by the ninth century, the Picts had all but disappeared, and their territories had gradually fallen under the influence of the Gaelic Kenneth MacAlpine, whose ancestors had come from Ireland.

This period of Scottish history, until the arrival of the Normans from France in the 11th century, is one of its blackest, and represents Scotland's own Dark Ages.

The Norman Invasion directly influenced the development of a Scottish character and identity, for rather than adopt Norman ways, many Northern English fled even further north and established themselves in Lowland Scotland. Their language became known for the first time as Scots. Among those refugees was the Anglo-Saxon Princess Margaret, who later married Malcolm III of Scotland, and devoted much of her life to re-establishing the church in Scotland.

However, Norman influence could not be resisted and a century later, in the 1300s, French was the official language of Court life, of the clergy and of the nobility south of the Celtic lands (largely the Highlands as we know them today), some of which were still partly occupied by the Norsemen.

Scotland could not consider itself a unified country under one king without the removal of the Norse presence. Then Alexander III grasped the dilemma by the horns.

He began to challenge the Norse presence in the Outer Hebrides, and in Orkney and Shetland, angering the Norse King Haakon, who retaliated by ordering an invasion of Scotland. Alexander and his troops met Haakon and defeated him at the Battle of Largs, where a peace treaty was finally signed. Alexander was known as the "peaceable king" and for the next few years Scotland thrived and prospered under his rule.

But peace was shortlived. When Alexander died in 1286 he left no successor, and King Edward I of England saw his chance for a takeover. Using the threat of force, he put his own man, John Balliol, on the Scottish throne. But when Edward called for Scottish support in his campaign against the French, Balliol turned against him. Not only did he refuse the call but, in a bold but foolhardy move, formed an alliance with the French against Edward.

Edward and his army rode into Scotland, bringing death and destruction and ravaging the land. He left behind him a maimed and broken Scotland. He also left with one of the Scots' most treasured national possessions, the Stone of Scone, on which Scottish kings had been crowned. (Sadly enough, the Stone has never been returned to Scotland permanently.)

However, a new hero was to give the Scots hope. Robert the Bruce (more French than Scottish – his name was actually Robert de Brus) gained much popular support and eventually had himself crowned king.

With Edward's death in 1307, Robert began to harass the English forces with guerilla tactics. It was inevitable that there would be an English reaction and it came in 1314, when 20,000 English militiamen massed against a mere 5,000 Scots at a place called Bannockburn.

It became an inspiring victory for the outnumbered Scots, who won against enormous odds, but they were unable to turn it into a real political advantage. It was 14 years before they finally reached agreement with the English, but by then too much had happened to allow any chance of a cordial Anglo-Scots alliance.

In 1320 an influential group of Scottish nobles and clerics gathered to formulate what became known as the Declaration of Arbroath. It was basically a statement of independence, of the right of the Scots to decide their own destiny, unfettered by London. To give it more impact, they sent a copy to the Pope.

The French Connection
In 1326, building on ties that John Balliol had forged with the French, the "Auld Alliance" between France and Scotland was formally established. It lasted for centuries, and through it Scots fought beside Joan of Arc, lined up with the French in the Hundred Years War against the English, and sought refuge in France from English oppression. So close was the relationship that at times it was said: "He that will France win, must with Scotland first begin".

These developments could have only one possible effect: to drive a wedge between the English and the Scots. It has not entirely disappeared even today.

After Robert the Bruce, and the brief reign of the ineffectual David II, Bruce's grandson became king. Known as Robert the Steward, his accession to the throne signalled the revival of a national identity, and the country flourished. It also had another significance: it was the start of the royal line that was to play such an important role in the affairs of Scotland – the Stuarts.

The fifteenth century saw a buoyant Scotland. Trade and commerce expanded, many monasteries were built and three universities – more than existed in England at the time – were established: St Andrews (1412), Glasgow (1451) and Aberdeen (1495).

But fortune did not smile in the same way on the monarchy. After Robert, James I was assassinated in 1437; James II, whose reign began when he was six, was killed accidentally by an exploding cannon, and James III, who came to the throne at the age of nine, was also the victim of assassination.

With James IV, hopes rose once more. Quarrels with England seemed to have been patched up and the future relationship between the two countries assured when James married Margaret Tudor, sister of Henry VIII. But James, an impetuous extrovert, quarreled with Henry (not the easiest of men to deal with) and while his brother-in-law was away fighting the French, James launched an invasion of England. But it was ill-conceived and badly prepared. It ended in death and a major defeat for James at Flodden in 1513.

All that had been gained at Bannockburn, almost exactly two centuries earlier, was lost in a moment of folly and stupidity.

James V succeeded to the throne and cemented Scotland's continuing relationship with France, marrying, first, the daughter of Francis I of France and after her death, Mary of Guise. The latter bore him a child (whom James survived by only a few hours), a daughter who was to become perhaps one of the most tragic figures of history – the future Mary Queen of Scots.

While her mother ruled Scotland as Regent, Mary spent most of her childhood in France, was raised as a Catholic and married the French Dauphin. In 1561, a widow, she returned to Scotland to succeed her mother. But Scotland wasn't ready for Mary. Under the stern, puritanical influence of the Calvinist John Knox, the Scottish parliament had recently denounced Catholicism as extreme and corrupt, and had proclaimed Protestantism as Scotland's faith.

Now they were faced with a Catholic monarch who further angered her subjects by marrying twice more; first to Darnley (murdered in 1567), then to Boswell. Opposition grew too much for her and she fled to London, where Elizabeth regarded her as a threat to the English throne and had her imprisoned in the Tower of London. She was beheaded in Fotheringay Castle.

James VI, the son of her marriage to Darnley, succeeded to the Scottish throne. He had two distinct advantages – he was Protestant and also heir to the English throne, which he inherited on Elizabeth's death in 1603. He became James I of England, and James VI of Scotland.

And so the stage was finally set for a rapport between the English and the Scots. But it wasn't meant to be. James virtually abandoned Scotland and, when he tried to insist on English-style church services and hymnals in Scottish churches, the Scots, led by the single-minded Knox, resisted.

The struggle resulted in deadlock, and the whole dispute was put aside when the English found their time occupied with a Civil War between the Royalists and Cromwell's Parliamentary forces. The wily Scots saw their chance to further their cause by fighting beside Cromwell and helping him win at Marston Moor. For their support in overthrowing Charles I, Cromwell granted the Scots their Covenants – guarantees of the right to worship as they wished.

But then even Cromwell went too far for the Scots. He beheaded Charles I. The Scots reacted by crowning his son, Charles II, on condition that he also guarantee the Covenants. Charles was forced to flee when Cromwell invaded Scotland. But his return was not long delayed and, on the Protector's death, Charles inherited the English throne, too. This measure was one of the first steps towards the Act of Union which, in 1707, established Scotland and England as one nation, with one parliament, established Protestantism as the national faith and ended forever any real possibility of a Catholic Stuart's accession to the throne.

This didn't stop the Catholic Stuarts from making two determined attempts to overthrow the Act – the Jacobite risings of 1715 and 1745 – after the Protestant Stuarts had been replaced by Protestant Hanoverians. In 1745, Charles Edward Stuart – Bonnie Prince Charlie – took Perth and Edinburgh, defeated the English at Prestonpans, and with pipes skirling and drums beating, marched as far south as Derby, some 180 miles into England. The English Court was panic stricken and had even made plans to evacuate London when the Scots suddenly retreated.

The Scots were finally beaten at Culloden by the Duke (known as "The Butcher") of Cumberland. The prince escaped the terrible retribution exacted by the English – the Highland Clearances, disarming of the Clans and banning of the tartan – by fleeing to France, where he died 43 years later.

By that time, the Jacobite cause, if not forgotten, had receded far enough into history never again to pose a threat to England or the new, emerging Anglo-Scots relationship. But the unnecessarily cruel and vindictive nature of the English reaction to the uprising was never forgotten, and even now many Scots recall the memory of those days with bitterness.

It may not be an exaggeration to say that the several popular movements for Scottish nationalism since then, culminating in the heady but temporary parliamentary successes of the 1960s, have roots going back to 1745. Nevertheless, since 1745 Scotland's history has been completely intertwined with England's.

But what of the land that has seen such a bloody history of its own?

City Dwellers
Including its 787 islands, Scotland covers about 30,000 square miles – more than one-third of the total mass of Great Britain. The population is widely scattered, but a third of the people live in just four cities: Glasgow (about a million), Edinburgh (half a million), Aberdeen and Dundee (about 200,000 each).

Scotland is traditionally divided into the Highlands and Lowlands, both historically and topographically. The Highlands are the part of the country originally occupied by the Celts. The dividing line between the two sections runs from Peterhead to the southwest border of Scotland, around the Firth of Clyde.

The islands are: the Inner Hebrides (of which Skye is the best known); the Outer Hebrides (including Harris and Lewis); Orkney, Shetland, and the islands of the Firth of Clyde (Arran and others); and of the Firth of Forth (among them Bass Rock). Most of them are inhabited only by sea birds. Less than 150 are home to man.

Glasgow is Scotland's oldest city – there was a settlement at a ford over the River Clyde as far back as AD 500. In the 17th and 18th centuries it was a wealthy market town, and its architecture was widely praised throughout Europe. The Clyde had not been dredged into the major waterway it is today and was still, in the words of Moray MacLaren, ". . . a lowland salmon stream. Around the city by the ford were rich gardens . . . and fruitful farms" (*Shell Guide to Scotland*, Ebury 1965).

Now, of course, it is a major industrial city and seaport. Its size and power are largely the result of a dynamism generated all over Britain during the Victorian era.

The elegant university, a landmark at the top of Gilmorehill, is evidence of this. Built in the 1870s by Sir George Gilbert Scott, it looks dreamily over the western rooftops of the city. The cathedral, which stands on the site of a chapel built by St. Mungo in AD 500, is the only surviving pre-Reformation Gothic structure on the Scottish mainland. The vaulted crypt is one of the best of its kind anywhere in Europe, and the well, in which St. Mungo is said to have performed baptisms, still attracts visitors.

The oldest house in Glasgow stands in Cathedral Square. Provand's Lordship, built in the 1470s, is now a museum. The center of the city is usually accepted to be George Square. It's a gathering place for pigeons, earning for the Square and surrounding streets the nickname, "Dodge City". Along with Catholicism and Protestantism, soccer is a major religion in Glasgow. Hampden Park stadium, with a capacity of nearly 150,000, is one of Europe's largest. There are two dates in the Scottish soccer calendar when all three religions come together, the days when Glasgow Celtic meet Glasgow Rangers. Celtic fans are predominantly Catholic, Rangers mainly Protestant, and although there have been occasional ugly clashes, peace is by and large maintained.

The city is within easy reach of beautiful countryside. Loch Lomond, for instance, the largest enclosed lake in Britain, and nearby Ben Lomond, a mountain which offers some superb views from its 3,200-foot summit, an easy and worthwhile climb. To the northeast lie the beautiful wooded hills of the Trossachs, immortalized by Scott in his famous poem, *The Lady of the Lake,* and also by Nathaniel Hawthorne in his *English Notebooks.*

In the direction of the Grampian Mountains, the Braes of Balquhidder provide some of Britain's best camping country. It was here that the legendary Rob Roy MacGregor led the English a merry chase before the 1715 uprising. He is buried near the ruined church of Kirkton.

Travelers through the Grampians are rewarded by superb scenery at places like the Devil's Elbow on the Cairnwell Pass, the highest main road in Britain. This is skiing country and over the past ten years, ski and après-ski facilities have been greatly improved. Glenshee and Aviemore, in the Cairngorms, offer a huge variety of winter sports facilities such as indoor ski schools, curling rinks, skating, tobogganing and – in summer – pony trekking, rock climbing and sail boarding.

Between the Grampians and the Cairngorms – the highest mountain range in Britain, with several peaks second only to Ben Nevis – lie Braemar and Balmoral on Deeside.

Royal Scotland
Braemar is probably best known today for its celebrated Highland Gatherings, but in 1715 it was where James Edward Stuart first raised the Jacobite banner to herald the Stuart uprising.

The Highland Games have been held at Braemar since 1832, and since Queen Victoria graced them with her presence in 1848 the games have enjoyed royal patronage. The Games consist of piping competitions, tugs-of-war, highland wrestling and dancing, and tossing the caber (which should, according to some experts, be pronounced "cabber"). The word caber means a branch from a tree. In early days it was literally that, with side shoots and leaves removed for the event. There is no standard size, and the point of the event is to throw the caber end-over-end.

The castle at Balmoral is the private residence of the Queen. Prince Albert bought it for Queen Victoria in 1852, paying the princely sum of £31,500 for it. He had it re-modeled with granite quarried right on the 24,000-acre Balmoral Estate. The castle is beautifully situated by the Dee, and although glimpses of it can be caught from the road it is sufficiently secluded to afford the Royal Family its necessary privacy.

The road to Tomintoul – the highest Highland town – winds through the sometimes forbidding Pass of Ballater, extremely narrow in places, and frequently blocked by winter snows. Eventually it wanders into Tomintoul, centered around a village green. The nearby valley of the Avon (pronounced "A'an") is regarded by many as one of Scotland's most beautiful glens.

North of Tomintoul is Speyside, one of the major whisky distilling areas, with Dufftown at its center. Rome was built on seven hills, so the local saying goes, but Dufftown stands on seven stills.

There is more lore and legend connected with whisky than any other Scottish institution. It has its own mystique which canny Scots are careful to perpetuate, with the result that the drink is one of Scotland's major exports. The first record of whisky appears in 1494, but authorities agree it was probably drunk long before that. It is defined as "a spirit obtained by distillation from a mash of cereal grains turned into sugar by the fermentation of malt." There have been many second-rate imitations, but the real thing is in a class by itself. Robbie Burns took it with water, sugar and lemon; Queen Victoria topped her port with it; the purists drink it neat, or with a dash of loch water, but never, never with ice!

The most beautiful approach to Aberdeen is by the coast road. "The one haunting and exasperatingly lovable city in Scotland", as it has been called, stretches elegantly between the Rivers Don and Dee. It is also known as the Granite City, much of it built from local granite mined at Rubislaw, which at 465-feet is the world's deepest quarry. Quarrying has been one of the city's major industries for many years, and Aberdeen granite is found all over the world – in sidewalks, graveyards, office buildings and other places where solid permanence is needed.

But oil is king in Aberdeen today, and you are reminded of its presence under the gray waters of the North Sea by the trappings of the industry visible from virtually every street corner. Plush oil company buildings, fleets of tankers, survey offices and a new crop of leisure centers, bars and restaurants provide oilmen with plenty of ways to spend their money.

Although declining, the fishing industry is still a major employer in Aberdeen, and the daily early morning fish market is a reminder of the city's heritage and is well worth a visit.

Local history is preserved in the Provost Skene's House, the oldest part of which dates from 1545. Within the city the Aulton, or old town, of Aberdeen, belongs for the most part to the University. It has become a stylish mixture of the best of the old with tasteful new student buildings.

Butcher's Battlefield
The road runs north through Forres, where Shakespeare set the "blasted heath" of *Macbeth* fame, and on towards Culloden, the burial ground of Jacobite hopes in 1746. A memorial stone mound marks the site where the English forces, under William, Duke of Cumberland, took just 40 minutes to rout the Stuart rebels. During this brief battle, Cumberland undoubtedly committed unnecessary acts of brutality, but he returned to great acclaim in London, where the flower "Sweet William" was named after him. To Scots, however, the flower has always been known as "Stinking Willy".

Skirting Inverness, and running southwest, are the menacing waters of Loch Ness, in some places 750 feet deep. What lurks in those depths? No one knows, but one thing is certain: as long as people want to believe in the existence of a monster the gloomy loch will continue to interest them. If the monster's existence is ever disproved, Loch Ness might fall into comparative obscurity.

Inverness, "the gateway to the Highlands", is also considered the Highland capital, housing many administrative offices for such Highland activities as forestry, deer hunting and small farming.

Urquhart Castle, overlooking the western shore of Loch Ness, has been a ruin for nearly 300 years and much of what now remains dates from 1509. There are two unopened vaults. It is said that one contains treasure, the other plague-infested clothing. But no one knows which is which and, not surprisingly, no one has ever tried to find out.

Dingwell, the former county town of Ross and Cromarty, was for many years a Norse town and the name comes from the Norse word "thing", meaning parliament.

Farther north, past Invergordon, where a section of the Royal Navy mutinied in 1931, is the attractive, ancient Royal Burgh of Tain. As the birthplace of St. Duthac, it has been a site of pilgrimages for many years. It is also where the wife, sister and daughter of Robert the Bruce were betrayed to their English pursuers. The Collegiate Church there dates back to the 14th century, and there is an interesting prison, housing a curfew bell, presumably used by the English to enforce regulations at the time of the Highland Clearances.

The original structure at Bonar Bridge, over the

Dornoch Firth, was designed in 1811 by Thomas Telford, one of England's great engineers, after the Meikle Ferry disaster in which 100 people were drowned.

Dornoch, once the county town of Sutherland is, according to Michael Brander, "a medieval town and on top of that a medieval cathedral town . . . something of a surprise." (*Around the Highlands,* Bles 1967). The cathedral is now the parish church and contains an unusual organ presented to the church in 1907 by the Scottish-American philanthropist, Andrew Carnegie.

Gothic Mistake

Farther up the coast lies Golspie, a fishing village and small resort town within easy reach of the beautiful Dunrobin Glen. And a mile to the north is the strangely-designed Dunrobin Castle, seat of the Dukes of Sutherland.

The present building which, says Michael Brander, appears to be "all minarets and turrets, a Gothic mistake", is mainly 19th century. Its contents, rather than the structure itself, are the chief attraction. Part of the castle is open as a museum, housing a collection of mementos gathered by the family through generations, both at home and abroad.

Wick lies on the coast road to John o' Groats and, like Dingwall, there is evidence of its Norse ancestry. The name comes from the Norse for "bay". The Old Man of Wick, today just a square stone tower, was in its heyday an impregnable castle perched on rocks overlooking the sea, and was probably built by the Norsemen. It's a bustling town with a market and an airport serving the major Scottish cities as well as Orkney to the northeast.

John o' Groats is called the most northerly point of Britain. However, it is not. That disinction belongs to Dunnett Head, to the west. John o' Groats itself is little more than a sprinkle of white-washed cottages, a hotel, some shops (including the inevitable souvenir stores) and a signpost pointing south that bears the legend "Land's End – 874 miles".

John o' Groats is named after a Dutchman, one of three brothers who ran the ferry to Orkney in the 16th century. According to the story, when they and their families numbered eight, a disagreement broke out over who was in charge. The only solution was to build an octagonal house with eight doors so that each member of the family could enter by his or her own door and sit at the octagonal table inside without taking precedence over any other. Sadly, the house has long since disappeared.

Between John o' Groats and Dunnett Head, and barely visible from the road, is the Castle of Mey, built in 1567 and now the private retreat of Queen Elizabeth, the Queen Mother.

From Dunnett Head, with its fine sweep of sand, can be seen the Islands of Orkney. There are 67 in all, of which about 20 are inhabited. Mainland is the largest. Its capital, Kirkwall, is 900 years old, with roots in the Norse tradition, and has all the appearance of a Scandinavian town. Stromness, the other main settlement on the island, is much more Scottish. It was a Celtic fishing village until mainland Scots started using it as a port for trade in the 17th century. Hudson Bay Company vessels used to call there regularly too. Now it is content, and quieter, as a small local fishing community.

The second largest Orkney island is Hoy, with a range of spectacular rocky peaks that makes it superb climbing country. The most challenging to the climber is the Old Man of Hoy, a vertical column of basalt rising 450-feet straight up from the western edge of the island. It has been scaled by only the most accomplished of climbers. There is plenty for the historically inclined on Hoy, including an Early Bronze Age tomb known as the Dwarfie Stone. Indeed, nearly all the Orkney Islands are rich in prehistoric artifacts. The Islanders are mainly farmers, and the fishing industry is rare, although visitors find the inland lochs abundant in brown trout.

The Shetland Isles are 60 miles northeast of Orkney.

Once you get beyond Unst, the most northerly of them, there is nothing but endless ocean between you and the North Pole.

There are about 100 islands in the Shetlands, some 20 of which are inhabited. Mainland is the largest, with Lerwick, its capital, a maze of narrow streets. It is a cosmopolitan town, often host to fishing crews from Russia and Japan, as well as western Europe. The North Sea oil boom has brought to Lerwick, as it has to Orkney, the personnel and paraphernalia of oil exploration.

One festival with indelible Viking links takes place in Lerwick each January. This is Up-Helly-Aa, an advance welcome to the arrival of the summer sun following the short days and long darkness of winter. Unlike Orkney, Shetland is mainly a fishing community, but it is also the home of the world famous Shetland ponies, bred on the 25-square-mile island of Fetlar. Shetland wool is also a major industry for the islands.

Back on the mainland, and continuing west along the north shore of Caithness, the stark whiteness of the atomic energy reactor at Dounreay appears on the landscape. Opened in 1960, it was one of Britain's first atomic reactors, a herald of the new nuclear age.

Highland Sport
But just a few miles south, on the moors of Caithness around Altnabreac, lies country that for years has provided the field and stream sports of Scotland, a real slice of the country's heritage: hunting, shooting and fishing, Scottish style.

The Thurso river provides excellent salmon fishing, there are many hill lochs for trout, and on the moors, grouse shooting, deer hunting and falconry.

Grouse are peculiarly Scottish: the Red, found on higher ground, and the Black (the male in fact is ebony and purple with a splash of crimson on his head), near woodland. They are protected for much of the year, but the Glorious Twelfth – of August – heralds the new shooting season, and many of England's leading restaurants go to elaborate lengths to serve the first grouse of the year.

Across the northern stub of Scotland, heading for the west coast, lies the beautiful, unspoiled Strath Naver, its peace and tranquility belying its stormy history, when small farmers and their families were forcibly evicted from the fertile land in the infamous Highland Clearances. At the southern end of the valley lies Loch Naver in a bowl in the hills. On its northern bank are two rundown, but preserved, 19th century farming townships, Grummore and Grumbeg.

The aptly named Cape Wrath is well known to sailors. Its rugged cliff face rising 400 feet out of the sea, with dangerous reefs below, can be seen from nearly 30 miles. A lighthouse beams out a warning message to seamen.

To the south lies Ullapool, now a fishing village and tourist center, but once a major port for the Scots emigrating by the thousand to North America at the time of the Clearances.

In some parts around Ullapool live strict sects from within the Free Kirk of Scotland who on Sundays, for instance, remove their tourist bed and breakfast signs, do no washing, and refuse to buy (or sell if they are shopkeepers) milk, food, newspapers, fuel and so on.

Among the most popular attractions on the west coast are the tropical gardens of Inverewe, thriving in the mild, damp climate of Wester Ross, close to the warming Gulf Stream and enjoying more than 60-inches of rain a year. At any time the gardens are lush with vegetation, and imported plants such as Monterey Pines, eucalyptus, and Australian tree ferns grow just as happily as they do in their native soils.

Skye, the most northerly of the Inner Hebrides and the largest of the Western Isles, has its own lore and legend and a very distinct personality of its own. Watching the sun setting over the Outer Hebrides islands of Harris and Lewis from Skye is an unforgettable experience. Just 50 miles long, with the mysterious Cuillin Hills in the south, the island seems to have a permanent bluish light of its own, except on those very rare, perfectly clear days.

It is mountainous throughout, with the Trotternish range in the north, where you can see the vertical stack or rock called the Old Man of Storr, and the strange rock formation of the Quiraing. Dunvegan Castle, dating from the ninth century, is the seat of the Macleod Clan, and is also a major attraction on the Island. Skye people are as gentle as their soft Highland accents, and with tourism restricted by the limited accommodation available, Skye has remained unspoiled and its hospitality unrivaled.

A few miles to the south lies the Island of Rum, now largely a center for the study of the large Red Deer population and, consequently, not always accessible to the traveler. To the east of Rum lies Eig (pronounced "egg"), a 24-square mile paradise for the botanist and naturalist. A wide range of plant life flourishes there as well as several species of animal life peculiar to the island.

The remaining islands of the larger Inner Hebrides are Raasay, where Johnson and Boswell stopped on their celebrated Highland tour; Rona, which is virtually uninhabited lies between Skye and the mainland; and the islands of Muck, Jura, Islay, Coll, Tiree, Colonsay and Canna.

Anglers' Delight
To the northwest are the Outer Hebrides, consisting of Barra, Eriskay, South and North Uist, Benbecula, Harris and Lewis.

The 1,500 inhabitants of Barra live by farming and fishing and are not reliant on tourists. Three-mile long Eriskay is where Bonnie Prince Charlie first landed from France in 1745, and it retains much lore and legend from that time, with an especially fine heritage of folk songs.

South Uist has a population of about 2,000 (largely farmers), and a tradition of producing the finest pipers. It is only 22 miles long but packed into that length are no less than 190 freshwater lochs – a delight for trout fishermen. It was on South Uist, just a few months after setting foot on Eriskay, that Bonnie Prince Charlie sought refuge after the battle of Culloden and from where he was rescued by Flora MacDonald.

North Uist is much more Norse in character and exclusively Protestant, in contrast to Catholic South Uist. It has many standing stone monuments and, a rare claim in the Hebrides, abundant numbers of salmon and trout. However, the island of Benbecula, probably the flattest of the Outer Hebrides group, is also an angler's dream.

Harris and Lewis are actually connected although they are described as islands. However, they are intrinsically different. Harris is mountainous, rocky and almost exclusively a fishing community where both the English and Gaelic spoken are, to the discerning ear, different from that spoken on Lewis which lies just 30 feet away across a small connecting bridge.

Lewis is larger, flatter and less appealing scenically but Moray McLaren has no doubt that "even among the highly individual Celtic community, the Lewis folk are remarkable . . . exhilarating." Lewis is a Gaelic stronghold and Stornaway, its capital, with its bustling, business-like manner, epitomizes the Gaelic character. Weaving, farming and fishing occupies most of the island's population of 20,000. The world-famous Harris tweed comes from both islands, but far more is made on Lewis because a greater percentage of its population is employed in the production of the fabric.

The beauty of the Hebrides, says McLaren, "lies in the spaciousness of sea and sky and land, with their long stretches of sand in which gold and a silvery-white mingle to greet the long Atlantic rollers. In the people of the outer isles still flourishes the essence of Scottish Celtic Gaeldom."

Back on the mainland, and heading south from Strome Ferry, the road leads past the romantically-situated Eilean Donnan Castle, one of the most photographed of all Scottish castles. It stands on a promontory of Loch Duich and overlooks the point where Lochs Alsh and Long join Duich. The structure dates back to the 12th century, but was virtually blasted out of the loch in the 18th century when an English man o' war sailed into Duich and fired broadsides into the castle, forcing the surrender of the Jacobite supporters within; a feat which had previously proved impossible to achieve by land attacks.

Through the Forest of Glenmoriston, where the Redcoats sought long and in vain for Bonnie Prince Charlie after the battle of Culloden, the road leads down to Fort William, nestled snugly below Britain's highest peak, Ben Nevis. Fort William, established as one of a line of frontier forts to control the Highlands in the 17th century, is now essentially a Victorian town. The old fort was demolished and completely rebuilt to accommodate the arrival of the railroad in 1864.

Ben Nevis rises 4,406-feet, but with its rounded top lacks the impact of lesser peaks. It can be comfortably climbed by the more active tourist on the gentle slopes from Achintee, a round trek that takes about eight hours. But on the other side, the northeast face offers even experienced climbers a real challenge.

The road to Spean Bridge provides spectacular views of Aonach Mor (4,000-feet) and the great corries of Ben Nevis. Spean Bridge was the site of one of the first battles in the 1745 Uprising, and was also a commando-training center during World War II. A dramatic memorial commemorates this fact. Here, too, as at several spots in the Highlands, there is an excellent tartan warehouse.

The tartan was first recorded in the 13th century and is thought originally to have denoted where the wearer lived, rather than clan or name. But the kilt did not catch on until George IV popularized it in the 1820s; before that the tartan was usually worn wrapped around the body in lengths of up to 16-feet, and in earlier days had to be removed before battle.

Brooding Glen

Cut back inland, around Loch Linnie, and ahead lies Glencoe. "Glencoe is undeniably beautiful," writes Michael Brander, "in a fearsome, rugged way, but I know of no glen in Scotland with a greater atmosphere of gloomy, brooding grandeur." Even, one might add, at the height of the tourist season. Then buses deposit visitors by the hundred, and gypsy heather-sellers ply their wares, and pipers fresh from Glasgow play a skirl or two (pipers who probably have never been farther north than Glencoe). Despite all this, the Glen seems able to retain the indelible, gloomy atmosphere created for it by the terrible massacre of 1692, when at least 40 of the Glen inhabitants of the MacDonald Clan were killed by English soldiers under the ignominious command of a Scot – Campbell of Glenorchy.

The clan system – the word derives from the Gaelic meaning family – no longer controls the affairs of the country. At the last count there were some 80 recognized clans (including those with some very un-Scottish names such as Rose and Arbuthnott – but no Scotts or Stewarts).

The Campbell war cry was "cruachan" and the mountain of that name lies beyond Dalmally, guarding the Pass of Brander that leads west to Oban. Ben Cruachan's highest peak soars to 3,689 feet but can be scaled by the reasonably fit. Traditionally, after the Oban Ball, the participants make an early morning climb of Cruachan before a hearty breakfast.

Oban, on the west coast overlooking Mull, is an attractive town of some 3,000 people. Its busy harbor, used by fishing vessels and MacBrayne steamers headed for the Isles, is overlooked by MacCaig's Folly. A circular, stadium-like structure, the building was started in the 1890s by a wealthy and eccentric bank manager, MacCaig, who intended it to be a museum. But when he died during the course of its construction his dream died with him.

Iona, off the south west of Mull, is famous worldwide. It was to this charming island that St. Columba brought Christianity in AD 563. The Abbey, restored around the turn of the century, holds regular services, and visitors from everywhere come to attend them and to see the work of the Iona Community which was founded in 1938 to maintain the old monastery ruins and the burial place of the Scottish kings. The island itself is a delight, seemingly as untouched and unspoiled as when St. Columba arrived.

The other side of Loch Awe from Oban is Inverary, the seat of the chief of the Campbell Clan, the Duke of Argyll. Inverary Castle is one of the chief attractions for the visitor to this delightful town, but it has been ravaged by fire throughout the years. In 1877 there was considerable fire damage and almost 100 years later a more widespread blaze broke out, resulting in the loss of many fine works of art and the closing of the castle to the public.

Going up through Glen Croe to Loch Fyne there used to be a steep climb, and at the top of the pass there is still a stone plaque inscribed "Rest, and be thankful". Many a walker of old was pleased to do so.

Once through the pass, Glasgow is almost within sight, and the traveller is again back in the Lowlands.

Edinburgh, only 30 miles east of Glasgow is, according to its inhabitants, a world apart. It has elegance and style. Princes Street compares with anything Europe has to offer, and the 1,000-year-old castle perched high above the town is a delight to the eye.

The city developed at the beginning of the 19th century and until the 1850s simply consisted of the buildings of the Old Town grouped around the Castle on the Rocks. St. Margaret's Chapel, built in 1076 and containing so much of Scotland's history, the Canongate Tolbooth, John Knox's House, the Palace of Holyroodhouse, Parliament House (now the Scottish Law Courts), and the Register House are just a few of the places any serious visitor must include in his itinerary.

In the wild Holyrood Park stands Arthur's Seat, a superb 822-foot panoramic vista atop a natural hill. The Edinburgh Tattoo, a fine demonstration at the floodlit Castle of military marching by pipe and drum bands, and the Edinburgh Festival, offering much that is best and new in the arts, are two annual events that bring thousands to this most attractive of cities.

Border Country is the land of the River Tweed which, for more than ten miles, actually defines the border between England and Scotland. For that reason it has a special place in Scottish hearts. Sir Walter Scott spent the last 20 years of his life at Abbotsford on its banks. Its waters nourish the rich pastures of the area, its salmon and trout are among the finest, and it feeds the prosperous Border towns of Peebles, Melrose and Kelso – where the tweed fabric is produced.

The border itself runs from near Lamberton on the east coast to Gretna Green. Now discreetly marked by simple road signs, the border nevertheless remains to many Scots the most important one they will ever cross. It can be a highly emotional moment, returning to Scotland, as even many non-Scots have found. Though Scots may leave home, Scotland never really leaves their hearts.

Charles Murray captured the feeling in verse when he wrote:

"Scotland our mither – since first we left your side,
From Quilimane to Capetown, we've wandered far and wide;
Yet aye from mining camp an' town, from koppie an' karou
Your sons richt kindly, auld wife, send hame their love to you."

Previous page: a crisp autumn day at Loch Moy. Above: Dunvegan Castle, home of the Macleod of Macleod, which has stood on the wild shores of the Isle of Skye for at least four centuries. Top: the castle of Eilean Donnan. Left: the tiny, crowded harbour of Pittenweem, one of the most picturesque Royal Burghs in the country. The small port is, without doubt, the heart of this ancient town.

Above: a shallow stretch of water, fringed by marshy land, lines the bottom of Glencoe. Facing page: (top left) the silky waters and snow-brushed heights of Sgurr Fhuaran contrast with the empty croft (bottom right) and wave-pounded coasts (top right and bottom left) of the Orkneys. Overleaf: two fine aerial views of the Royal Burgh of St Andrews.

Top left: a well-fleeced flock of black face sheep graze some of the grassland to be found on the moors of northern Scotland. On the west coast of Hoy Island, one of the Orkneys, can be found the Old Man of Hoy (centre left). At 450 feet, this is the tallest rock stack in the British Isles and can be seen from the mainland. Bottom left: part of Loch Eilt, which stands along one of the more beautiful stretches of the Road to the Isles. Left: the tumbling waters of the River Coe dash across the rocks and boulders as they rush to escape the 'Glen of Weeping'. Above: the picturesque lighthouse of Gourock, a fine yachting centre on the Firth of Clyde. Overleaf: (left) a cluster of small fishing boats in Aberdeen harbour and (right) the Caledonian Canal at Corpach, where the canal descends 'Neptune's Staircase', a series of eight locks.

Facing page: a view across Gigha Island, the small, flat, fertile island which lies off the coast of Kintyre, and which can only be reached by steamer from West Loch Tarbet.

Above: Fort Augustus, where the Caledonian Canal can be seen descending a ladder of locks to reach the dark waters of Loch Ness, which reach into the distance beneath snow-capped mountains.

Above: the rays of the sinking sun streak Blaven, on the Isle of Skye; perhaps the loveliest of the Inner Hebrides. Facing page: the pale, yellow light of evening silhouettes the gaunt ruin of Kilchurn Castle, whose keep was erected in 1440 by Sir Colin Campbell as a refuge for himself and his family during the violence and warfare of the Scottish fifteenth century.

Left: a fine aerial view of Abbotsford, the best known home of Scotland's most famous novelist, Sir Walter Scott. Scott was greatly interested in Scottish traditions and history, as evidenced in his writings, and Abbotsford was built in the Scottish Baronial style to suit its owner. Above: the tiny crofting community of Tarskavaig, on the Isle of Skye. Top: the massive, rounded peaks that rise above Glencoe.

33

Eilean Donnan Castle (above) was built by Alexander II in 1220 on an island in Loch Duich, the causeway was added centuries later. Facing page: (top left) a winter view of Glen Orchy; (far right) the ivy-clad ruins of Castle Kennedy, which was burnt out in 1715; (bottom centre) scenery around Glen Etive and (bottom left) the solid, stone railway viaduct at Glenfinnan blends into the natural scenery.

At 4,406 feet Ben Nevis, seen (above) from Banavie, is the tallest mountain in Britain and its summit can be reached by a stony footpath from Glen Nevis, though on occasion motor cars have been driven to the summit. Facing page: a view north along the Noust of Bigging Bay on Mainland in the Orkney Islands, as Atlantic rollers pound dramatically onto the rocky shore.

Left: an aerial view of Inverness, showing the city centre, railway yards and the fine new suspension bridge which carries the modern road across the narrows between Beauly Forth and Inner Moray. The new link north to Dingwall replaces the old A9 which wound miles inland to avoid natural obstacles. Top: Loch Eil. Above: the 'Fair City' of Perth, an ancient Royal Burgh whose past is filled with historic fights, murders and rebellions. Overleaf: (left) cranes and docks on the Clyde at Glasgow and (right) a solitary yacht on the still waters of Loch Creran at sunset.

The snows of winter grip Scotland more firmly than any other part of Britain, as shown (above) in Glen Etive, whose river runs down to the sea loch of the same name. Loch Tay (facing page) is a fifteen-mile-long freshwater loch renowned for the quality of its salmon fishing. From the loch's eastern end flows the River Tay which, by the time it reaches the sea, has the greatest volume of any British River.

Top: a highland stag. Above: the Palace of Holyroodhouse in Edinburgh. Right: the 13th century Urquhart Castle and Loch Ness. Far right, bottom: Mid Yell, one of the ports where the mail and passenger steamer stops along the coast of Yell, in the Shetlands. Far right, top: a bridge near Loch Oich, in the Great Glen.

Above: the small harbour of Ayr, topped by the slender spire of the Town Buildings, is best known for its connections with Robert Burns. Facing page: the peat-laden River Dochart. Overleaf: (left) the small fishing village of Plockton, on an inlet of Loch Carron and (right) the ruins of Castle Moil, on the Isle of Skye, rise above the harbour of Kyleakin, whence the ferry leaves for the mainland.

Above: the River Dochart tumbles down its valley. Facing page: (top left) a loch in Glen Etive; (bottom left) river and mountains in northern Argyll; (top right) the setting sun over Loch Eil and (bottom right) a sparkling burn and springtide flowers at Aberfeldy.

Left: the two bridges across the Firth of Forth replaced the ancient ferry which had plied the waters for centuries. The great cantilevered rail bridge was built between 1883 and 1890 and was held up as one of the world's greatest feats of engineering when it was first completed. The two main spans each cover 1,710 feet, while the centre span of the modern road bridge is 3,300 feet long, with side spans of 1,337 feet. Above: a battered trawler puts out to sea from Aberdeen. Top: a rowboat moored beside Loch Eil. Overleaf: Kilchurn Castle (left), long the home of the Breadalbane family, was garrisoned by Hanoverian troops during the rising of Bonnie Prince Charlie in 1745, which began when the Prince landed at Glenfinnan (right).

Above: the scenic Loch Tummel, which in recent years has been dammed and extended, though a fish ladder has been installed to allow fish to climb into the loch. Facing page: Loch Arkaig.

Overleaf: (left) the well-protected harbour of Pittenweem and (right) the town of Tobermory, named after the well of St Mary is the largest resort on the Isle of Mull.

On a lonely moor to the northwest of Spean Bridge stands the poignant memorial (above). It was erected in memory of the commandos of World War II who trained in this area and was designed by Scott Sutherland in 1952. In 1745, just to the west, a skirmish took place which marked the start of the Jacobite rising of that year and three days later Prince Charles Edward Stuart raised his standard in the beautiful setting of Glenfinnan (right), having arrived from exile in France. Many clans flocked to the cause and followed the standard south into England and to eventual ruin at Culloden, though some fought just as ferociously against the Stuart cause. The tower, topped by a statue of a highlander, was erected in 1815 by Macdonald of Glenaladale. Top right: the magnificent sandstone ruins of Jedburgh Abbey, perhaps the finest of the abbeys along the Borders. Centre right: a tiled cottage in Pittenweem. Bottom right: the turbulent River Dochart.

Facing page: Glencoe, the site of the infamous massacre of 1692, when a Campbell took advantage of a royal order and royal troops to pay off an old score with the Macdonalds. The troops enjoyed the hospitality of the Macdonald clan for a week before treacherously falling upon their hosts and killing them in their beds. Above: the monument at Glenfinnan commemorating the clansmen of the '45.

Top: Loch Laggan, whose natural beauty was greatly changed with construction of the Lochaber Power Scheme. During the work some ancient dugout canoes were found in the loch. Above: the fishing fleet of Kinlochbervie on the sea loch of Loch Inchard, on the mainland side of the Minch. It was near this town that a mermaid was supposedly seen earlier this century. Left: Perth, with the squat spire of St John's Church (centre of picture) where John Knox delivered his famous sermon against idolatory in the church.

Facing page: (top left) the romantically sited ruins of Kilchurn Castle on the shores of Loch Awe; (top right) the sun sets over Eilean Donnan Castle; (bottom left) Loch Garry and (bottom right) the

A82 loops its way through Glencoe on its route from Tyndrum to Fort William, whence came the troops to perpetrate the infamous massacre. Above: rugged cliffs of Esha Ness, on the Shetland Islands.

Left: Loch Ness contains the greatest volume of freshwater of any British lake. It is also said to contain a monster. References to the beast go back to AD 565, when St Columba saved a Pict from a 'monster' in the River Ness. In the centuries which followed the Loch earned an evil reputation among the locals, but it was not until the new main road was constructed in the 1930s that the loch earned international fame. Photographs and sightings by reliable witnesses built up an impressive array of evidence to indicate the presence of at least one large animal in the loch. But since neither solid remains nor a specimen has been recovered, the monster remains a mystery. Above: the Caledonian Canal at Fort William, at the southern end of the loch. Facing page: a fine aerial view of Edinburgh in winter.

Above: grey evening settles on the still waters of Loch Eil, while a
golden glow spreads across the face of Loch Leven (facing page).

When the Wolf of Badenoch came to Elgin in 1390, he found a prosperous town and a beautiful cathedral, both of which he put to the torch. The cathedral was rebuilt, but by 1807 had fallen into the ruin that it is today (top). Above: a cottage in Glencoe. Right: the elegant mock-Gothic Culzean Castle, built in 1777, which is one of Robert Adam's finest works. Overleaf: (left) the gaunt ruins of Kilchurn Castle, of which Wordsworth wrote 'Child of loud-throated War! the mountain stream roars in thy hearing; but thy hour of rest is come, and thou art silent in thy age', and (right) the Glencoe Massif.

Above: the scattered community of Finstown on the Bay of Firth on Mainland, the largest of the Orkneys. The village is famed for prehistoric structures; the Gallery Grave of Rennibister, burial mound of Maeshowe and broch on Damsay Island all being notable examples of their kind. Facing page: Tarbert is the main base for the important Loch Fyne herring industry.

Above: one of many Scottish castles which have fallen into decay and ruin as the violence of clan society has given way to the peaceful ways of the twentieth century. Facing page: the dashing waters of the River Beathach run through a snow-tinged landscape in Glen Orchy.

Right: the gaunt ruins of Castle Campbell. Known originally as Castle Gloom, it was built in the 14th century by the Earl of Argyll. It was later visited by John Knox in 1556 and Mary, Queen of Scots, before being besieged by the Marquis of Montrose during his brilliant campaign of 1645. Above: Loch Rannoch. Facing page: Loch Morlich.

Above: Loch Garten. Facing page: (top left) the Shetland town of Scalloway, once the home of the notoriously cruel Patrick Stewart, Earl of Shetland, who is said to have mixed blood into the mortar of his castle and who was executed in 1615; (top right) Stirling Castle; (bottom left) the ruined Melrose Abbey, where the heart of Robert the Bruce is buried and (bottom right) Glencoe.

These pages: the two bridges across the Firth of Forth. They connect the two towns of Queensferry, which took their name from the ferry now replaced by the bridges, which was used by Queen Margaret on her journeys between Edinburgh and Dunfermline.

Encouraged by David I's widespread ecclesiastical reform, a group of monks came from Alnwick to a loop in the Tweed some miles south of Edinburgh. Here they founded Dryburgh Abbey, whose fertile lands made it rich, but whose strategic position laid it open to constant border raiding. A particularly violent attack in 1544 reduced it to the ruins that survive today (facing page). In recent years the Abbey has become a tourist attraction as it holds the remains of Sir Walter Scott and Field Marshal Earl Haig. Autumn (right) and winter (below) each bring their special magic to the scenery of Loch Moy. Bottom right: Lochan Fada. Overleaf left: the modern Inverlochy Castle, which replaced the structure near which, in 1645, the Marquis of Montrose gained one of his greatest victories by means of forced marches through the mountains. Overleaf right: Loch Leven.

Above: the lonely, dark ribbon of the A93 winds through the snow-covered landscape of Glen Shee, between Braemar and Blairgowrie.

Facing page: Schiehallion rises to some 3,547 feet above the waters of Loch Rannoch, much enlarged by its modern dam.

Facing page: Urquhart Castle on Strone Point above Loch Ness. The site was fortified by the semi-independent Lord of the Isles during the 13th century, but most of the buildings to be seen today belong to the 16th century stronghold of the Chief of Grant. The castle has featured in some of the best known photographs and sightings of the Loch Ness Monster. Above: a typical forest scene in the Highlands.

Facing page: the tiny harbour of Brodick, on the Isle of Arran, which is served by the Clyde steamers. The peak of Goat Fell, which dominates the bay, was the site of a famous and unexplained death last century. Above: Ben Vorlich.

The ancient city of Edinburgh (left) has been intimately involved with the history of Scotland for centuries, passing from hand to hand and sharing in the nation's varying fortunes. The castle rock has been defended since at least the 6th century, though its earliest history is only preserved in half-forgotten legend and romance. The jumble of the mediaeval city, which cluster, around the long road known as 'the Royal Mile' (centre of picture), contrasts with the 'New Town' of Georgian elegance to the north and the even more modern housing estates which surround both. Above: Drummond Castle, Crieff, has been much rebuilt after being bombarded by Cromwell and partially dismantled during the '45. Left: Caerlaverock Castle, whose stormy history under the Maxwells first made its massive defences necessary and then smashed them into ruin.

The mighty wind which brought down the Tay Bridge in 1879, and thereby caused some execrable verse from the pen of William McGonagall, also brought down one of the towers of Kilchurn Castle (facing page). Above: Loch Ness in solemn mood.

Above: the still waters of Loch Moy reflect the mountains beyond. Facing page: (top left) Loch Garry; (top right) a small boat beached beside Loch Unagin; (bottom left) the tumbling waters of the Falls of Bran near Dunkeld and (bottom right) Loch Leven. Overleaf: (left) the gloom of evening over Whiteness Voe and (right) St Margaret's Hope, on the north coast of South Ronaldsay in the Orkneys.

This page: (left) Dunbeath Castle, a largely 19th-century building around a 15th-century keep, which fell to Montrose in 1650; (top left) Cawdor Castle, where King Duncan is said to have died; (top right) the harbour at Oban, backed by a hill crowned with McCaig's Folly, a curious circular structure intended as a museum but never finished and (above) Loch Long. Facing page: the Glenfinnan Viaduct.

The natural defences of Edinburgh Castle (above) have been so improved upon by man that it is only known to have fallen twice in all its long and turbulent history; once in 1296 when Edward I of England captured it and again in 1341 when the Scots took it back again. Facing page: an aerial view across the Georgian crescents of the New Town towards the Salisbury Crags and Arthur's Seat.

107

Far left: the low-lying land around the settlement of Kennacley on South Harris in the Outer Hebrides. The windswept, bleak scenery is typical of much of the island. Left: the Grey Mare's Tail, one of Scotland's highest waterfalls, lies just to the northeast of Moffat. The massacre that took place in Glencoe (above) in 1692 was tragic but hardly unprovoked, for the McDonalds had engaged in feuds as much as any other clan. A grave at Lochearnhead records one of their attacks on Ardvorlich House. Overleaf left: the fortress of Stirling Castle. It was in an effort to reach the English garrison of the Castle that England's Edward II led his army to disaster on the banks of the Bannockburn. Overleaf right: fertile land on the Isle of Bute.

109

On a hill high above the Clyde at Greenock stands the massive memorial (above). Symbolically combining the Cross of Lorraine with an anchor, this monument was raised in memory of the Free French sailors who gave their lives in the Second World War to keep open the sea lanes trade across the Atlantic. Facing page: sunset brings a soft, golden light to water-meads south of Renfrew.

Above: Loch Moy. Facing page: (top left) the granite mass of Ben Nevis, at 4,406 feet the tallest mountain in Britain, stands reflected in the waters of Loch Linnhe; (centre left) the Crinan Canal; (bottom left) the bridge across the Teith at Callander; (bottom right) Crieff, which suffered damage in both the '15 and the '45 and (top right) the clear blue waters of Loch Faskally.

Top: a steamer from the mainland docks to deliver goods, mail and passengers at a pier on the Isle of Jura, with the aptly-named Paps of Jura rising beyond. Above: the western entrance of the Crinan Canal, which was built during the Napoleonic Wars to take ships from the Clyde to the Atlantic without the need to round the Mull of Kintyre. Dumfries (left) has, perhaps, more history than any Scottish town of comparable size. It was here that Robert the Bruce stabbed the Red Comyn, here that Robert Burns wrote much of his work and is buried. The town suffered badly at the hands of Bonnie Prince Charlie during the '45.

Dating back to the days of the Picts, the stoutly defensive broch of Gurness (facing page), at Aikerness on Mainland in the Orkneys, is surrounded by ruined outbuildings. Above: the fine harbour at Aberdeen, which can handle large, modern ships. Overleaf: (left) Dumfries and (right) a modern road bridge and older railway viaduct cross a river in the Eildon Hills.

Previous pages: (left) a
firework display over
Edinburgh Castle and (right)
the bridge across the mouth
of Loch Etive at Connel.
These pages: (far left, top)
the harbour at Lerwick in
the Shetland Islands; (far
left, bottom) the town of
Oban seen from its harbour;
(left) Princes Street,
Edinburgh, from the Castle
walls; (top) the centre of
Aberdeen and (above)
Paisley's Victorian Town
Hall.

Above: the herring port of Mallaig lies at the western end of the Road to the Isles and is the terminal for ferries to the islands. Facing page: (top left) Loch Achnacarry; (top right) fishing boats at Pittenweem; (bottom left) the bay of Portree, largest town on Skye, and (bottom right) Loch Lochy in the Great Glen. Overleaf: (left) Scone Palace and (right) St Monance.

127

Above: Castle Stalker stands on its lonely
island in Loch Laich, an inlet of Loch Linnhe.
This fine example of the Scottish tower house
was built around 1500 by the Stewarts of Appin
and has the Royal Arms of James IV carved over
the entrance. The tower house is a peculiarly
Scottish form of defence, being cheap and
imposing and ideally suited to the raids and
feuds of clan warfare, where only small armies
were involved. Right: the sun sets over a sea
loch. Top right: Eilean Donnan Castle, on its
island in Loch Duich, was bombarded by a British
frigate during the abortive Jacobite rising of
1719. Centre right: Inveraray Castle. Far right:
Urquhart Castle, on the shores of Loch Ness.
Overleaf: two fine aerial views of Glasgow,
which dates back to a chapel founded about AD
500 by St Mungo.

Facing page: the summit of Ben Nevis rises above Loch Linnhe and Fort William. The fort, after which the town is named, was built in 1655 by General Monk, and resisted Jacobite attacks during both the '15 and the '45. Above: a typical, small Highland village.

Sir Walter Scott was so captivated by the romance and legends of historical Scotland that when he came to build himself a home at Cartleyhole he first renamed it Abbotsford and then proceeded to construct a fabulous house of turrets and castellations (above). Right: the rocky slopes of Glencoe. Far right: the world-famous Gleneagles Hotel and its golf links, which are a Mecca for golfers from around the world.

Above: a drum major and pipers in full dress on the Esplanade of Edinburgh Castle. Facing page: (top left) the massive Tay Road Bridge, completed in 1965, crosses the Firth of Tay at Dundee, one of the towns stormed by Montrose in 1645; (bottom left) Kyleakin, named after a king of Norway who sailed through the narrows in 1263, and (right) the monument at Glenfinnan.

Above: the noble pile of Floors Castle. The building was originally designed by Vanbrugh in 1718, but later modifications have changed the character of this Kelso mansion. Facing page: the Royal Burgh of Rothesay, on the Isle of Bute, with its beach and amenities, is one of the best-known resorts on the island. The town gives its name to the Dukedom of Rothesay, held by the Prince of Wales.

Autumn shades the trees and the braken-covered slopes which rise up to blend with the snow-sheathed and cloud-enshrouded heights above Loch Tummel.

Some died in their beds at the hands of the foe,
Some fled in the night and were lost in the snow.
Facing page: the snows of Glencoe in which many McDonalds perished.

In 1848 Queen Victoria and Prince Albert visited the Balmoral Estate. The Queen was so enamoured of the place that her consort purchased it four years later and rebuilt the house in the Scottish Baronial style. It has remained a favoured Royal residence ever since. Above: the golden rays of the setting sun over Loch Laggan. Left: Ben Nevis from Tulloch.

145

Facing page: the ancient city of Perth on the banks of the Tay.
Above: a steamer running down Loch Linnhe from Fort William.

Overleaf: (left) a view of the River Tay from Kinnoull Hill near Perth and (right) Loch Voil and the Braes of Balquhidder.

Above: Scalloway lies on the west coast of Mainland in the Shetland Islands and was the ancient capital of the islands. It retains the justiciary to this day, though the official capital is Lerwick, to the east. Facing page: Scaraster Bay, on South Harris.

Above: Crinan Harbour, one of the more popular yachting resorts on the Sound of Jura. Top: the scenic glories of Glen Etive, in the lonely mountain fastness of the Grampians. Although one of the oldest of Scottish cities, Dundee (left) is also amongst the most modern. The new road bridge across the Firth of Tay reaches into the heart of a city which is now a complex of gleaming new buildings. But Dundee has not lost its past nor its links with William Wallace, Montrose, General Monk, Admiral Duncan and Anna, Duchess of Monmouth.

153

Above: Inveraray Castle, seat for five centuries of the Duke of Argyll, head of the clan Campbell, who is known to his clansmen as the MacCailean Mor, son of the great Colin. Facing page: rich grazing land at Strath Mashie. Overleaf: (left) the small herring port made up of the two Royal burghs of Anstruther Easter and Anstruther Wester and (right) the violet shades of evening at Loch Linnhe.

The highly indented coastline of Scotland has long made travel difficult, but modern construction techniques have made it possible to bridge the firths and sounds of the nation: (facing page) the road and rail bridges across the Tay at Dundee and (above) the road bridge across the Firth of Forth at Queensferry.

159

INDEX